Long Road Ahead Without Him

A Collection of Thoughts & Poems

K. H. THOM

Long Road Ahead Without Him

A Collection of Thoughts & Poems

All rights reserved. This book or any portion thereof may not be reproduced or used in any manner whatsoever without the prior express written permission of the author and publisher.

First edition

Text copyright © K. H. Thom

Poems copyright © K. H. Thom

Front cover photograph copyright © K. H. Thom

Back cover photographs copyright © K. H. Thom

Photograph of Judy & Connie copyright © K. H. Thom

Copyright © 2024 K. H. THOM

All rights reserved.

ISBN: 9798329650716

DEDICATION

For Sylvia with my love.

CONTENTS

	Acknowledgments	i
1	JIMMY.	1
2	MY PETS.	7
3	CATHY.	11
4	HOLDING ON TO OUR HUMANITY.	13
5	TAKING OUR TIME.	17
6	LOVE, FAITH & FRIENDS.	21
7	TRUE LOVE.	25
8	LOVE GOES ON.	29
9	FINAL THOUGHTS.	33
10	MY GIRLS.	34

ACKNOWLEDGMENTS

All my love and thanks must go to Jimmy. I would never have written this book were it not for him. He was my everything. I miss him every day.

Thank you to my beautiful Mum and Dad for their unfailing love and for everything that they have done for me. I know that thanks can never really be enough but I do thank them with all my heart and I love them both so very much.

A huge thank you to my friend, Evelyn, for proofreading for me yet again and for all her help whilst Jimmy was ill and when he passed away. She really is a star.

A special thank you to Chris for helping to give me confidence by encouraging me to share the poems which I had scribbled down in my notebook since Jimmy had passed away.

Thank you to Max and Sylvia for always wanting to hear them and for all their love and support.

Thank you to everyone who has encouraged me to keep on writing.

Thank you to Judy and Connie for faithfully sitting beside me each time I put pen to paper.

I give all thanks and praise to God for all that He has given me. For the precious years that I spent with Jimmy and for the love that we shared.

1 JIMMY.

My husband, Jimmy, passed away on 25th July 2022 and life, as I knew it, has changed irrevocably. Grief is a very personal journey. It has to be as no two people are the same. I say this now, at the beginning, as, should anyone read this book, I have no wish to be misinterpreted as someone who has any special authority on grief because I haven't. Every day someone, somewhere loses someone that they love. I write this purely as a way to try to articulate my own thoughts and feelings. The days and evenings are long without him and often, in the absence of someone to talk to, I find that writing has become the next best thing to speaking my thoughts out loud. My pen and paper are never very far away and are invaluable as my close confidante. This small collection of poems is my tribute to the man that I love and it also includes some of my thoughts as I journey through my grief.

Jimmy was a quiet man, a man of few words, but when he did speak it was always worth listening to. He was a thoughtful, perceptive man and an attentive listener. He carried much within himself. He was my rock, my friend and my everything. Someone very close to us described us as soulmates and I believe we were. During the sixteen years that we were married we were pretty much always together. Many couples need time apart from each other and, as I've said, we are all different, what works for one person is just no good for another, but, for us, being together made us both happy. Sixteen years is a long time and yet it seemed to go so fast and so I am thankful that we were able to spend so much of it in each other's company.

We lived a quiet life which revolved around our home and our garden. Tending our garden and caring for each other and our little family of pets was the greatest part of our life together. Whilst it may be seen by some as rather dull it certainly wasn't because it was a life full of love and I have so often given thanks for it, both whilst Jimmy was still alive and since he has passed away. To observe him in the garden was, undoubtedly, to observe him at his best. I wrote the poem below just before our 10th wedding anniversary.

The Gardener.

To see him in his garden
is to see him at his best.
For his body is at ease
and his mind is quite at rest.
And his heart is free to wander
through the borders that he tends.
Many plants he's known from seedlings,
have now become his friends.
He has an eye for colour
and a leaning toward beauty.
This quiet and modest man
with a steadfast sense of duty.
One of nature's gentlemen,
a gentle nature through and through.
He's faithful and dependable,
his heart is always warm and true.
Blessed with an artist's hands,
to fashion living things,
there's a special kind of peace
that being with him brings.
His eyes are filled with light
and it seems to shine so clear,
through his careful observations
and his will to persevere.
He says little, but sees everything,
so much is held within.
Oh, for a cup of the patience,
so freely bestowed upon him.
It takes years to gain his wisdom.
A garden needs time to form and grow
and the tender care of the gardener,
through whom God's love may flow.
Keeping rhythm with the seasons,
through rain and wind and sun,
beats the steady and contented heart
of a man whose work is well done.

Long Road Ahead Without Him.

We were always close and, when Jimmy fell ill in December 2017, it hit us both very hard. We endured it together. As time went on, he gradually became more and more frail and, on a couple of occasions, he had to go into hospital for a while. The place where he should have received the most help and understanding turned out to be quite the opposite for him. I spent a night feeling uneasy about him, although, at the time, I thought that it was just me being over-anxious.

Feelings of Unease Whilst Jimmy was in Hospital.

People tell me I must rest,
but I can't rest when you're not here.
You are the man who holds my heart,
the soul my soul needs to be near.
Being married means being together,
we live, we love, we share,
and tonight, I feel you need me,
and yet, I am not there.
I'm feeling very tired
and I know it's very late,
but if you were here and needing help
I know I would not hesitate
to try to bring you comfort,
or to help to ease your pain.
Oh Jimmy, Jimmy, Jimmy,
I sigh and say your name.
Three times I've been to the bathroom,
expecting you to be there,
but, of course, you're not,
and so, I turn, once more, to prayer.
I ask God to watch over you
I pray and pray so fervently,
that tomorrow, my James Thom,
you will come safely home to me.

Long Road Ahead Without Him.

When Jimmy did come home the next day, he told me that one of the night staff on the ward had been mean to him. He had told him to "move it" when he was taking him to the toilet and to "hurry up". Jimmy had difficulty breathing and was also partially disabled owing to his right foot having been crushed in an accident some years before. I was appalled. The poem below was written shortly afterwards.

If Man Continues to Evolve.

If man continues to evolve
I wonder, what will he become?
If he looks only unto himself
surely, his heart will grow numb?
When the sensitive soul is sneered at
and treated like a fool.
When the gentle heart is at the mercy
of those who would be cruel.
When the elderly feel unwanted
because no-one has the time.
Why should becoming old and frail
feel like it's some kind of crime?
When those who should be cherished
are treated with contempt
Will he feel he's beyond judgement?
Does he think he'll be exempt?
Jesus helped the helpless,
the wounded and the lame.
For the poor and the sick and the needy,
for each of **them**, He came.
And, even as He suffered,
He still reached out to me and you.
He said, "Father, forgive them,
for they know not what they do."
If man really wants to improve himself,
to find a better way to live,
then let him learn to love like Jesus
and be able to forgive.
Then no matter how tired he becomes
he'll be given the strength to care each day,
because faith in Jesus Christ means
Love will *always* find a way.

Long Road Ahead Without Him.

As our 16th wedding anniversary drew closer, I was in a quandary as to what to do. Jimmy was very frail by this time but I had the feeling that some kind of small celebration might help to lift his spirits and mine.

After much prayer and deliberation, I made the decision to purchase a small gazebo with windows and a door. With a great deal of help from my Mum and Dad and my friend, Evelyn, it was erected in our back garden. Mum did a wonderful buffet for us and I decorated it with a mixture of real and artificial flowers. We had a beautiful afternoon together. It was so good to see him smiling and I was deeply thankful.

Jimmy passed away two months later. I wrote the poem below a couple of days before our anniversary. It was also one of the poems which was read out at his funeral.

For Jimmy.

I talk a lot. Your words are few.
I moan a lot, you *never* do.
I rush, you *always* take your time.
So glad I'm yours and you are mine.
I cry. You rarely shed a tear.
I fret. You never show your fear.
You laugh whilst I am full of care
and, yet, we make a perfect pair.
You've been my rock, my friend, my love,
a special gift from God above.
A hug from you just makes my day.
I love you more than words can say.
Our life together has been full,
quietly lived, but never dull.
We've loved our pets, we've loved our flowers,
we've shared so many happy hours.
Tilly, Judy, you and me,
we've been as happy as can be.
Life changes but true love holds fast.
I know our love is made to last.
And I will love you all my days,
your gentle and unhurried ways,
that smile that fills your eyes with light
and warms my heart with loves' delight.

Long Road Ahead Without Him.

Thank you so much Mum and Dad.

I lost my Jimmy on a Monday
and it seemed that time stood still.
I had not thought that I would lose him,
though I knew that he was ill.
The call to say he'd passed away,
the guilt because I wasn't there,
to hold him and to kiss him
and to give him all my love and care.
Such a quiet and gentle man,
he suffered long without complaint.
When I got tired and cross at him,
he bore it bravely like a saint.
How I wished I were more like him,
that I might bear this awful pain,
the daily ache and night long yearning,
just to see him once again.
He was the great love of my life,
the man that taught my heart to sing.
I'm lost without my Jimmy,
he always was my everything.
Life feels torn apart and upside down,
my heart is broken and so sad.
Yet, I know it would be far, far worse,
if not for my loving Mum and Dad.
In this time of deepest sorrow,
I know I have been blessed
with a Mum and Dad who love me
and who always do their best.
For each time I fail to thank you both
for all the selfless things you do,
let me say it now, a heartfelt thank you,
Mum and Dad, I do love you.

I can never thank my Mum and Dad enough for always being there for me, but especially for all that they did when Jimmy passed away. They truly are the best parents anyone could ever wish for.

2 MY PETS.

Getting by without Jimmy is, like everything else, something I can only do through God's grace. Some days I do better than others. Maybe the closest thing we find to God's love, here on this earth, is the love of our pets. My birds and animals are a most wonderful source of joy and strength to me. Their love helps me to get out of bed in a morning and comforts me when I go to bed at night. As Jimmy's daughter, Joan, said to me just after he passed away – "It's the animals that will help to keep you going." She was right.

These poems are written with my deepest gratitude for their steadfast, unconditional love which helps to rally me again and again. They are my children, the family which Jimmy and I loved and cared for together and caring for them each day helps to give shape and meaning to my life, each of them are precious. They each have their own special gifts to impart and I am continually humbled by their devotion to me. As I write this now, my canary Hosea, is singing so sweetly and my cockatiel, Toby, is saying his name, my dog, Judy, is asleep on the settee beside me and my other dog, Connie, is lying across my feet and I know that I am very, very lucky.

My two dogs, Judy and Connie, are probably as close to me as anyone ever could be. We are pretty much always together. They sleep on my bed with me at night and the love that they give me is so very special. When our first dog, Tilly, came into our lives, Jimmy and I both felt that she helped to make our lives complete. She fitted in perfectly and quickly became part of us. After we lost Tilly, Judy came along and brought with her the comfort which only a dog can give. During the five years of Jimmy's illness, she was a great source of solace to us both. Connie came along six months after Jimmy passed away and has made a wonderful difference to Judy and to me. I just wish that Jimmy could have met her too. He loved dogs very much.

Long Road Ahead Without Him.

The Love of my Birds and Animals.

There are times when weariness
threatens to defeat me
and I'm ready to lie down
and just to let it beat me.
But then, my gentle Judy
puts her wet nose in my hand
and leans against my leg
to let me know she understands
and the look of love within her eyes
warms my heart in such a way,
that it humbles me to carry on,
to rise and face another day.
My erstwhile puppy, Connie,
presents me with her favourite toy.
Her face is filled with mischief
and her tail wags with pure joy.
And the guinea pigs are squeaking,
Irrepressible as they celebrate
the arrival of their breakfast,
even though I'm running late.
And Toby moves along his perch,
bows his head and says his name.
I tell him he's a good boy
and we play a little game.
But how do I articulate,
such a sweet and simple thing,
for the way my soul is lifted
when my canaries start to sing?
I give all thanks and praise to God
that even when I'm tired and down,
the love of my birds and animals
helps to keep me coming round.

Long Road Ahead Without Him.

The Love Beyond the Waterfall.

There's a waterfall that's teeming
and yet, it makes no sound.
There's a rock that's slowly crumbling
and falling to the ground.

But then the dawn begins to break
and I hear the blackbird's song,
somehow banishing the nighttime
which seemed so very dark and long.

The waterfall that was teeming
are the tears that no-one hears or sees
and the crumbling rock behind it,
well, it felt like that was me.

The aching loneliness of grief
sometimes feels too hard to bear
but a light shines through the darkness,
when we know that others care.

And my two dogs are beside me,
softly snoring, reassuringly warm,
steadfast in their company
as I ride my inner storm.

Long Road Ahead Without Him.

Giving Thanks for my Two Dogs.

It's that wet nose on my cheek,
that tongue that licks my ear
and, when I'm weeping,
tries to dry my every tear.

It's those eyes that look inside me,
right through to my soul.
They see me warts and all
yet still love me as a whole.

And each time I return home,
it's those ever-wagging tails.
A greeting so sincere, so full of cheer
that it never ever fails

To make me smile and make thankful
for all my blessings in this life.
For their love alters not
in times of joy or strife.

I may miss human conversation,
miss lots of things but then,
I know that I would never find
two better friends than them.

3 CATHY.

My friend, Cathy, passed away just two months after Jimmy died. We were very close, messaged each other almost every day. She had adopted me (unofficially) as her little sister. Our messages to each other invariably began with "Hi Sis" and ended with "Love you, Sis". Her death was a huge shock and, as with Jimmy, her passing has left a void which I'm still struggling with.

Cathy was an incredibly brave person who had suffered a great deal. Maybe one of the hardest things that she had to bear was the grief from losing her five babies. She had endured five miscarriages, losing four baby girls and a baby boy. She used to tell me that one of the things which hurt her deeply was that, because they were miscarriages, some people failed to see them as losing a child and this made her grief that much harder to bear.

Cathy talked a great deal about the children that she had lost. She told me that each year, when she went on holiday to Devon, she felt very close to them and could envisage them playing as she sat on a quiet stretch of beach there. The things that she described to me about how she watched them fishing in rock pools for crabs and pretty shells and building sandcastles together and how, at the end of the day, they would all slowly disappear from view but that her son, Andrew, would always turn and wave once more. These things inspired me to write the poem on the next page.

I miss Cathy very, very much but I hope that she is now reunited with her five children and that she no longer has to wave goodbye to them at the end of the day but is able to go home with them, that she is happy and at peace.

Long Road Ahead Without Him.

Watching Her Children at Play.

Andrew's standing on a rock.
Simone is knee deep in a pool.
The sun is warm upon their backs,
the water is so clear and cool
Natalie has pretty shells,
Eleanor has found some too.
The tide is slowly coming in,
the sky is just a sheet of blue.
A gull is soaring overhead,
the air fills with his haunting call.
The sandcastle the children built
is standing very proud and tall.
Christina shouts, she's caught a crab!
The others gather round to see.
They hold it up to show to Mum,
she waves back at them happily.
She hears their whoops of sheer delight,
she sees their joy in simple play
and says a silent prayer of thanks.
It has been such a perfect day.
They start to gather up their things.
Sadly, now it's time to go.
She whispers, "God bless. I love you,
more than you will ever know."
They wave at her with little hands
and she waves back with all her might.
She waves and waves and waves
until they're almost out of sight.
Straining to see them as they disappear,
along this peaceful stretch of shore,
her heart lifts momentarily
as Andrew turns and waves once more.

4 HOLDING ON TO OUR HUMANITY.

As anyone who has lost someone dear to them knows, there is a sea of paperwork to deal with and it comes at the time when we least feel like dealing with it. There are also numerous telephone calls to notify companies about the death of our loved one and, at the time, it seems never ending.

Maybe at this time, more than any other, we come to realise and appreciate the importance of simple humanity which ultimately binds us all together as human beings. Sometimes the absence of this humanity, at a time when we are already feeling lost and low, can be quite difficult to cope with.

It is standard practice these days that when we phone a company we are met with an automated response and are given various options of pressing 1 for this and 2 for that and so on and although we have come to expect it, it can still feel overwhelming and add to the turmoil within us which loss can bring.

I guess I'm only a lay person but I cannot understand why human beings seem to want to become less human and even, in some cases, make themselves completely surplus to requirement. Automated responses, self-service checkouts and so much is online now so that it is no longer necessary to see or speak to a human being. So many things which are "virtual" but not real. I have to ask, what is wrong with the personal touch? And why are we so eager to discard our humanity in favour of machines?

We have more forms of communication than ever before but the number of lonely people out there continues to rise. Often, these days, people do not know their neighbours. Is this really how man wants to evolve?

Long Road Ahead Without Him.

Response to an Automated Reply.

When we phone a company for help
we get an automated reply.
There is no warm response,
no-one that hears our desperate cry.

And no-one to say they're sorry,
nor to listen as we speak.
Just press one for this and two for that.
but none are really what we seek.

And their website gives little comfort,
just one more reason to groan,
leaving those who are forced to use it
feeling very much alone.

God has given us thoughts to share,
our hearts were made to love and care.
So why, oh why, don't we use them,
to help each other everywhere?

Or do we prefer the cold and impersonal?
Lack of humanity leaves a huge void.
Please, let us not be indifferent,
lest we slowly, but surely, become android.

Long Road Ahead Without Him.

Do We Know Our Neighbours?

We don't know our neighbours like we did when I was small.
There was a love beyond the garden fence that I so happily recall.

A special kind of fellowship based on giving and on sharing.
They were our extended family and life seemed full of caring.

I'm lucky to have known it, although I miss it now.
Some folk may pass the time of day but it's not the same somehow.

The warmth that I remember, seems diluted, almost gone.
Has life become *so* busy that we don't "know" anyone?

There are more forms of communication than we've ever had before.
Yet, the lonely people among us seem to number more and more.

And people die from loneliness without us ever knowing who they are
because we just don't have the time, or feel that we can't stretch that far.

Yet, Jesus' love is plentiful, enough for every single home,
that *all* may have their share and that *none* be left alone.

For those of us who have been blessed with the gift of faith there is the comfort of knowing that this is God's world, not ours and if we remain faithful to Him and keep His commands then He will remain faithful to us.

Beyond the Rainbow of Compassion.

Through the mists of grief before me
and the stirrings of my soul,
I see a brave new world,
where one day, I'll be whole.

The education of the heart
is slow and filled with pain,
where much seems at a standstill
and I don't feel any gain.

But all the time I'm growing,
like a seed deep in the earth
and the warmth of love is flowing
as I reach toward rebirth.

Until I stand within the light,
too pure for me to see,
where truth and love are calling
as they wait to set me free.

In a kingdom filled with kindness,
in the shadow of a gentle heart,
which may render all things tender,
mending all that's torn apart.

Though nothing can I offer
and nothing can I own,
beyond the rainbow of compassion
I will cease to feel alone.

5 TAKING OUR TIME.

There are so many things that I miss about Jimmy, not least for his quiet sense of calm, his gentle good nature, his innate patience which resonated itself in almost everything he did. Jimmy was not afraid to take his time and he steadied those around him. As his son, Andrew, once said – "If you're feeling stressed just spend half an hour with Dad and you'll soon start to feel calmer."

His will to persevere was paramount when it came to completing all tasks before him. One of his favourite sayings was – "Nothing is impossible, it just takes time is all."

Jimmy's will to persevere helped to save the lives of at least two of our guinea pigs. Bernard and Pip were both special needs guinea pigs who gained extra years to live thanks to Jimmy's patient perseverance when it came to syringe feeding them. They were both wonderful little characters but perhaps Bernard, in particular, seemed to reflect some of Jimmy's special qualities.

We seem to live in a world where man just wants to go faster and faster but we surely lose a great deal by doing so. Every day I miss Jimmy and his peaceful, unhurried ways which, I believe, were born of a gentle, loving heart and maybe we could each make a difference by just taking our time every once in a while.

Long Road Ahead Without Him.

A Quiet Man.

It's such a noisy, busy world.
It seems we're always on the go
and yet, there are still some,
who are willing to take life slow.

They carefully, patiently take their time,
to pause and to reflect,
to search for deeper meaning
and to steadfastly connect.

I knew a quiet man once.
He lived life at a gentle pace.
He always got things done
but his life was not a race.

He took the time to listen
and he was most discerning.
The effect that he had upon others
gave calm and stilled their yearning.

He slowed my step and steadied me
to persevere, to give my all.
He'd say, "Nothing is impossible,
it just takes time, is all."

In him I found an inner peace
and as I look back now, I see
this quiet and modest, gentle man
made *all* the difference to me.

Long Road Ahead Without Him.

The Things that Bernard has Taught Me.

To meet the world with a steady gaze
and a humble, gentle heart,
brings a sense of quiet fortitude
when life is rudely torn apart.

To simply keep on keeping on,
when all your energy is spent,
so that your comforter is comforted
and still feels you are content.

To always show you're thankful,
even for the smallest thing.
So that your giver may be given
a joy they want to sing.

To find peace on the worst of days,
when life seems fragile, hope seems frail,
and still be certain deep within you
that true love cannot fail.

These things I have been slow to learn,
they are not always plain to see,
but it's the things that really matter
that Bernard has taught me.

Taking Time for our Neighbour.

When our neighbour cries, do we pass them by?
Do we not have a minute to spare?
Will we cross the road? Will share their load?
Will we not take a moment to care?

Life is lived in haste, there's no time to waste
and we've troubles enough of our own.
Just a hand to hold is worth more than gold
if it stops someone from feeling alone.

If we build a wall, it will surely fall
if the base is not founded in love.
Every gardener knows, nothing truly grows
unless planted and tended in love.

Why not start today in a little way,
just reach out and tell someone you're there.
Right across this land, take your neighbour's hand,
make a difference by showing you care.

If it's love we choose we will never lose
and we may even gain a true friend.
Though it may take years, see beyond the tears,
love will heal, love will win in the end.

6 LOVE, FAITH & FRIENDS.

The power of God's love is never to be underestimated. I know that I would not have come thus far without it. So many times, when I have been feeling at my lowest ebb, the simple kindness of a friend or even, sometimes, of a complete stranger have helped to rally me once more.

When Jimmy and I were married the Bible reading during our wedding ceremony was taken from Corinthians chapter 1 verse 13. It has always been one of my favourite pieces of scripture but, when Jimmy became ill, the words took on a new significance for me. I clung to them each day.

Phone calls, text messages, letters and emails from family and friends help to keep me going during these difficult days. I am ever grateful to my Mum and Dad and my close friends for bearing with me. I thank them humbly for their love and care and I give thanks and praise to God for all love and goodness which comes from Him, for it was certainly not by my own strength that I continued to care for Jimmy as he became more and more frail.

Long Road Ahead Without Him.

Poem inspired by Corinthians Chapter 1 Verse 13.

Love is patient, love is kind,
all thought of self is left behind.
It does not envy, does not gloat,
does not keep itself remote.
Does not give or take offense,
nor does it seek recompense.
Bears no resentment, is not rude,
changes not with scene or mood.
Love is gentle, love is humble,
wants to help when others stumble.
Love is old and love is new,
cherishing all that's good and true.
When life is hurtling off the scale,
love stands firm, it does not fail,
still moves to trust and to forgive,
to love is the only way to live.

Friendship.

Friendship must be stronger
than the strongest thing on earth.
Friendship must last longer
than the oldest thing on earth.
Friendship must give more
than we are capable of giving.
Friendship must endure
way beyond our living.
Friendship must be *always* there,
in sunshine and in stormy weather.
Friendship **is** unceasing care,
a cherished love that lasts forever.
No matter if it's old or new
Friendship must be *ever* true.

Long Road Ahead Without Him.

Loving Kindness.

To face another winter
without him by my side
makes me want to hibernate
or, at least, to run and hide.

To brave the cold without him,
to hold, to hug, to cuddle,
to tell him of my troubles
when my head is in a muddle.

During long, dark winter nights
that seemed to last forever,
we kept each other warm,
we rode each storm together.

But, now, the worries are all mine,
storms that I must ride alone.
The constant stream of household bills,
the general running of the home.

But money is *only* money
and things are *only* things.
Friendship is more important
and all the joy it brings.

As there is a time to love,
so, there is a time to grieve.
And it means far more to give
than it does to receive.

Our achievements and possessions,
through learning and through knowing,
these things may help a little,
but loving kindness keeps us going.

Star of Love.

I have seen the Christmas star, shining in the sky.
I have seen the Christmas star, twinkling way up high.
The light that led the wisemen to the stable by the Inn,
to the Christ child in the manger, come to take away our sin.
Tiny hands, wee button nose, warm and cosy in the hay.
The wisemen and the shepherds came to worship where He lay.
I didn't see the Christ child, but I have seen His star
and His light is *ever* near me, though it's shining from afar.
The light that drew the wisemen draws me to Him now
and He's calling me to love and the time to love is now,
not tomorrow or the next day or in the coming year
but each moment that I'm given, for as long as I am here.
Jesus walks beside me. His light fails me never.
He teaches me to walk in love from now until forever.

7 TRUE LOVE.

Just as the words from Corinthians Chapter 1 Verse 13 helped to comfort and inspire me so too did the words from Shakespeare's sonnet 116. The love that I shared with Jimmy proved to be just as luminous and beautiful in difficult times as it had been through all the good years of our marriage.

The poems in this section are, unashamedly, about true love, about the great joy and sadness that it brings. For we cannot hope to know one without eventually knowing the other, they are each part of the same. We cannot have the joy without also knowing the pain. The deeper the love, the more intense the pain of loss but, as hard as it is, I wouldn't have wanted it any other way.

Sometimes the simplest of things can bring solace during dark and difficult times. Watching the geese fly over each day never failed to lift my heart. Knowing that they pair for life somehow helped me to feel closer to Jimmy after he had passed away.

Long Road Ahead Without Him.

One Special Person.

If you have one special person
who is there to take your hand,
someone who really loves you,
who you know will understand.

Someone who is beside you
on sleeping and on waking,
who wants to make you smile,
to hold you when your heart is aching.

Someone willing to shoulder your burden
who will gladly share your yoke
and still be there beside you,
even when you're stony broke.

Someone who *always* puts you first
and, happily, leaves themselves till last.
Who loves you as you are
and doesn't care about the past.

Someone whose heart is fixed on you,
because *you* are their one and only
and, so long as they are with you,
you will never ever feel lonely.

Someone who holds your dreams,
who truly helps your heart to sing.
If you have one special person,
then you do have everything.

Long Road Ahead Without Him.

Thankful to Have Known True Love.

Another day without him,
another day to face.
My world feels very empty,
a strange and lonely place.

There are so many, many things
that I'd still like to share,
so much I'd like to tell him,
if only he were there.

And the ache inside my heart,
it never goes away,
always I carry it with me,
try to brave it every day.

We did everything together
and we were so content
I'm grateful for the memories
of all the happy times we spent.

He used to hold me in his arms
and I held him when he was ill.
We were so very much in love
and, I know, I love him still.

Some hurts just run too deep
even when we've cried and cried.
My life changed irrevocably
the day my Jimmy died.

The hardest pain I've ever known
Yet, I do thank our Lord above.
For I am ever thankful
that I have known true love.

Long Road Ahead Without Him.

The Calling of The Geese.

I heard a distant honking sound
and then the geese came into view,
re-awakening within my soul
a faith in all that's good and true.
For I knew they were migrating,
as their great wings rose and fell.
Goodbyes are never easy
and so, I wished them well.
They teach mankind about true love,
when they pair, they pair for life.
The ever-loving husband stays
forever near his loving wife.
Their graceful beauty whilst in flight,
their amazing skills of navigation.
How *do* they *always* find their way?
The truth is hallowed information.
Each one is answering a calling,
ancient, wild and free.
It is beyond the laws of science
for they fly by God's decree.
They are part of His creation,
much of which is unexplained,
but the seeds He first imbued in them,
have faithfully remained,
to migrate and to procreate,
to rise, to fly high up above,
through the glory of His wisdom
by the power of His love.

8 LOVE GOES ON.

I feel so far away from Jimmy and, yet, I still feel close to him, here in the house that we lived in for the biggest part of our married life and most especially in the garden. We planned and planted the garden together and we shared so much joy there. I can be feeling pretty desolate but a few moments spent watering the plants in his greenhouse and I feel a sense of warmth and peace which kind of washes over me and leaves me feeling able to cope once more.

After we lost our first dog, Tilly, we both agreed that we could still feel that she was near to us. I believe that love goes on. It does not stop simply because we can no longer see each other. I don't pretend to understand it, I only know what I feel deep within my heart. Faith is believing in what we cannot see. We don't see love but we feel it, we know it's there and it is what makes this life worth living.

Love does not die.

Love You Still.

It's the empty space beside me,
on the sofa, in the bed.
The shoulder that is missing,
where I used to rest my head.
The hand I loved to hold
which sadly isn't there.
The calm you always gave me,
just by being there.
The love you gave so freely
in your steady, gentle way.
The smile that lit your eyes
and brought sunshine to my day.
The softness of your voice,
the wisdom in the things you said.
The quietness in your soul
and every fine thought in your head.
The life we shared together,
all the things we used to do.
The difference you made to me,
just by being you.
The love that changed my life,
I believe it still goes on,
unseen, yet ever present,
helping me to carry on.

Long Road Ahead Without Him.

Forgetting You Not.

Those free seeds from the magazine
that we planted years ago
began a tender love affair
that seems to grow and grow.

I behold a sea of forget me nots,
a mist of bright and beautiful blues
that shimmer in the evening light,
their soft, enchanting, faerie hues.

Mingling with the wood anemones,
blue and yellow, snowy white,
that magically appear each spring
filling me with great delight.

The lemony, creamy primroses
you planted with such care,
with their gentle, angel faces,
they are all still there.

And the daffodils and the tulips,
the enormous poppies, blousy pink,
all draw me closer to you
and they always make me think.

There are seeds growing in your greenhouse,
the first to be sown since you fell ill
and every inch of your workbench
in warmth and silence, bears you still.

Though I may feel I've lost you,
I see you are not really gone.
Through the garden we planted together,
the love that we shared lives on.

Long Road Ahead Without Him.

We don't give enough thought to grieving,
to the enormous sadness that it brings,
the lonely hours, the gaping void,
the way that it totally changes all things.

We just live on as best we can,
knowing life will never be the same.
Every day I talk to his picture,
every day I say his name.

I still have his clothes in the wardrobe,
I still have his books on the shelf.
All the tasks we once shared together
I must now do by myself.

Someone described us as soulmates
and I believe that it was true,
for he's always in my heart
and in everything I do.

It's a long road ahead without him,
one that I must travel day by day,
without sight, nor sound, nor touch of him,
but, somehow, love still leads the way.

FINAL THOUGHTS.

I do not imagine that very many people will read this little book but if just one person who is grieving for a loved one should read it and find some small measure of comfort within these pages then it will not have been written in vain.

MY GIRLS.

Judy and Connie - friends, comforters and confidantes.

ABOUT THE AUTHOR

K. H. Thom lives with her two dogs, Judy and Connie, her cockatiel, Toby, her two canaries, Snowy and Hosea and her two guinea pigs, Alfred and Danny.

She is also the author of -:

True Friendship Never Dies.
Gentle Words of Faith and Love.
At Christmas and Always.
Pinky & Horatio.

Printed in Great Britain
by Amazon